A WORLD OF ORIGAMI
EASY TUNDRA ORIGAMI

written by Jennifer Sanderson
origami by Jessica Moon

BEARPORT
PUBLISHING

Minneapolis, Minnesota

CREATE!

Credits

8, © PICARD Gweg/Shutterstock; 10, © Alexander Piragis/Shutterstock; 14, © FotoRequest/Shutterstock; 17, © Masianya/Shutterstock; 20, © Steve Sayles/Wikimedia Commons; 22, © Jukka Jantunen/Shutterstock; 22, © Henrik A. Jonsson/Shutterstock

Editor: Sarah Eason
Designers: Jessica Moon and Paul Myerscough

Library of Congress Cataloging-in-Publication Data

Names: Sanderson, Jennifer, author. | Moon, Jessica, designer.
Title: Easy tundra origami / by Jennifer Sanderson.
Other titles: Tundra origami
Description: Minneapolis, Minnesota : Bearport Publishing, [2022] | Series: A world of origami | Includes bibliographical references and index.
Identifiers: LCCN 2021003336 (print) | LCCN 2021003337 (ebook) | ISBN 9781636910840 (library binding) | ISBN 9781636913261 (paperback) | ISBN 9781636910918 (ebook)
Subjects: LCSH: Origami--Juvenile literature. | Tundra ecology--Juvenile literature.
Classification: LCC TT872.5 .S257 2022 (print) | LCC TT872.5 (ebook) | DDC 736/.982--dc23
LC record available at https://lccn.loc.gov/2021003336
LC ebook record available at https://lccn.loc.gov/2021003337

Copyright © 2022 Bearport Publishing Company. All rights reserved. No part of this publication may be reproduced in whole or in part, stored in any retrieval system, or transmitted in any form or by any means, electronic, mechanical, photocopying, recording, or otherwise, without written permission from the publisher.

For more information, write to Bearport Publishing, 5357 Penn Avenue South, Minneapolis, MN 55419. Printed in the United States of America.

Contents

A World of Origami 4
Arctic Fox 6
Tundra Shrub 10
Snowy Owl 12
Pasqueflower 16
Arctic Hare 18

About the Tundra 22
Glossary 23
Index 24
Read More 24
Learn More Online 24
About the Authors 24

A World of Origami

What Is Origami?

Origami is the Japanese art of paper folding. With the right folds, you can make all kinds of things, from arctic shrubs to snowy owls. Get ready to make a **tundra** world of origami!

Before you get started, there are a few key terms you'll need to know.

Origami Terms

Rotate Turn the paper.

Turn over Flip over the paper.

Cut Cut the paper along the line.

Mountain fold Bend the paper backward, away from you.

Valley fold Lift the paper and bend it toward you.

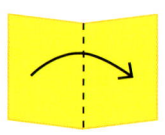

Pleat fold Fold the paper in one direction and then in the opposite direction.

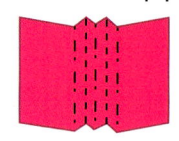

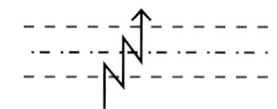

Squash fold Open two layers and then press them flat.

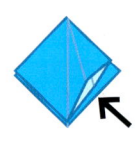

Inside reverse fold Push the tip of the paper inward and squeeze the paper together.

Outside reverse fold Open the paper slightly, fold the tip outward, and squeeze the paper together.

Blintz base fold

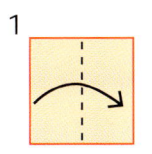

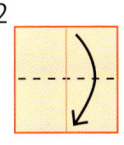

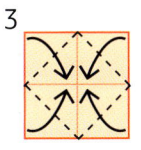

1 Valley fold, then unfold.
2 Valley fold, then unfold.
3 Valley fold the corners in to the center.
4 Done.

Kite base fold

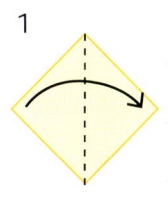

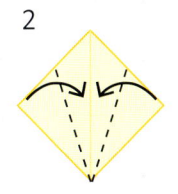

1 Valley fold, then unfold.
2 Valley fold the sides in to the center.
3 Done.

Square base fold

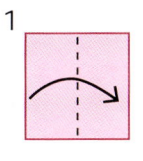

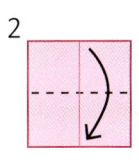

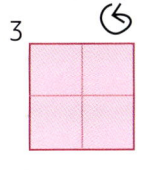

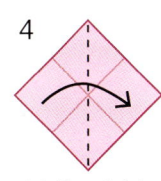

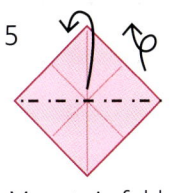

1 Valley fold, then unfold.
2 Valley fold, then unfold.
3 Rotate.
4 Valley fold, then unfold.
5 Mountain fold, then unfold. Turn over.
6 Make two inside reverse folds on opposite corners.
7 Press closed.
8 Done.

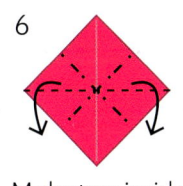

Bird base fold   Start with a square base, then follow these steps.

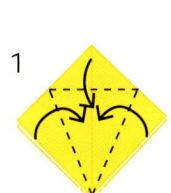

1 Valley fold three points in to the center, as shown. Then unfold.
2a Lift up the top layer, pushing the sides in as you do.
2b
3 Turn over.
4 Valley fold the sides to the center, then unfold.
5 Fold the top layer as you did in step 2.
6 Done.

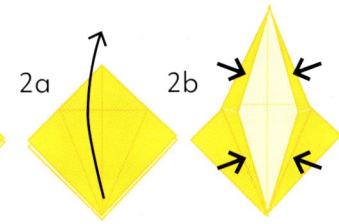

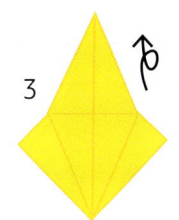

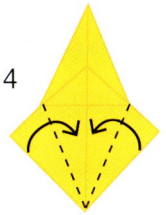

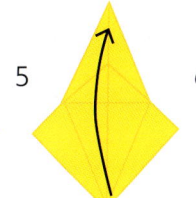

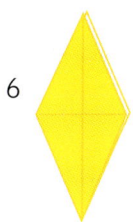

5

Arctic Fox

How does the arctic fox survive bitterly cold weather? Its thick fur helps keep it warm. When it gets really cold, the fox curls up. It tucks its legs and head under its body and behind its fluffy tail. Luckily, your folded friend won't have to worry about the cold!

1. Valley fold your paper in half from top to bottom, then unfold it.

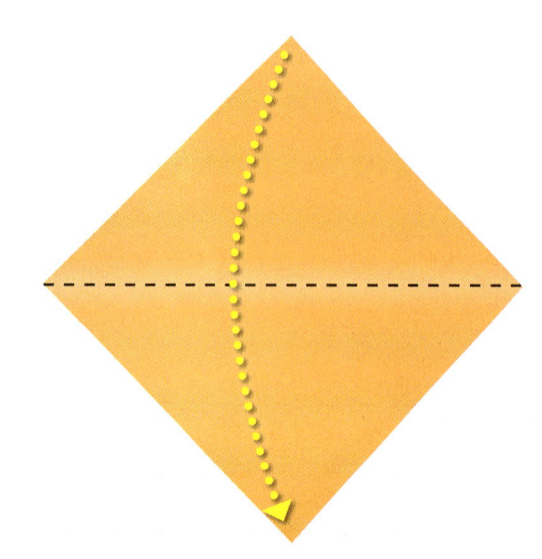

You will need
- 6 x 6 inch (15 x 15 cm) origami paper

2 Valley fold your paper in half from left to right.

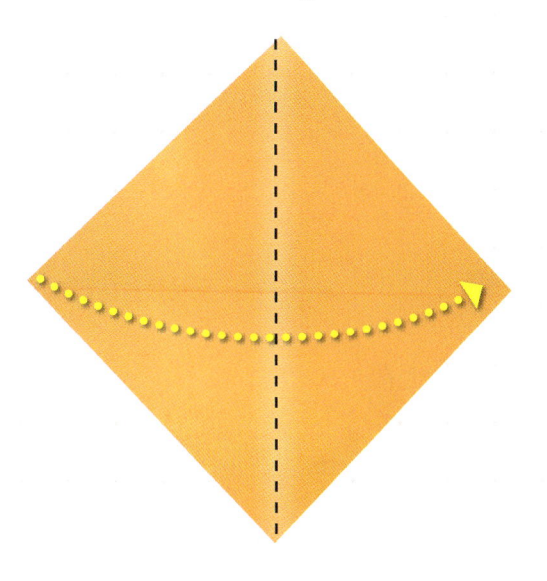

3 Valley fold the top and bottom points in to the center point.

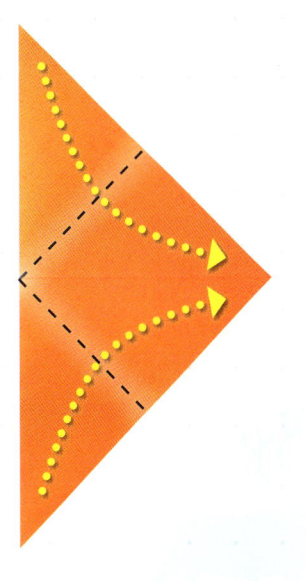

4 Mountain fold your paper.

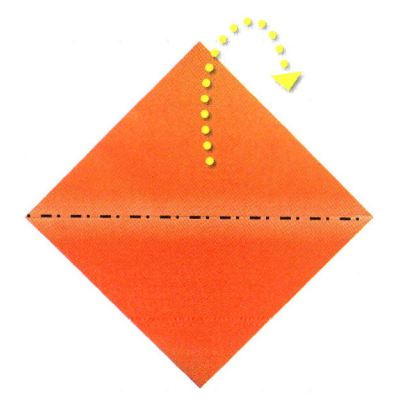

5 Valley fold the upper layer up and over to the left.

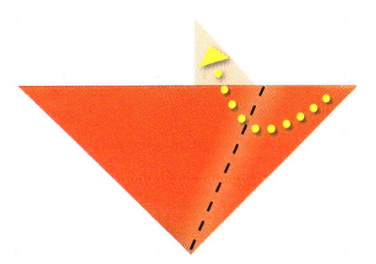

6. Your model should look like this. To create the face, lift up the next layer and make a squash fold.

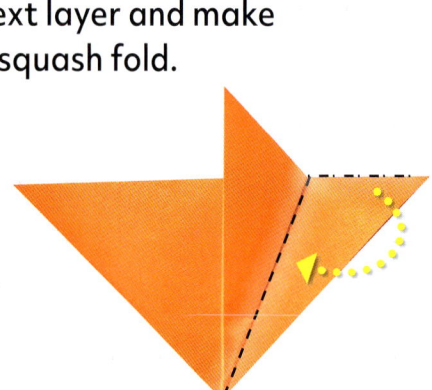

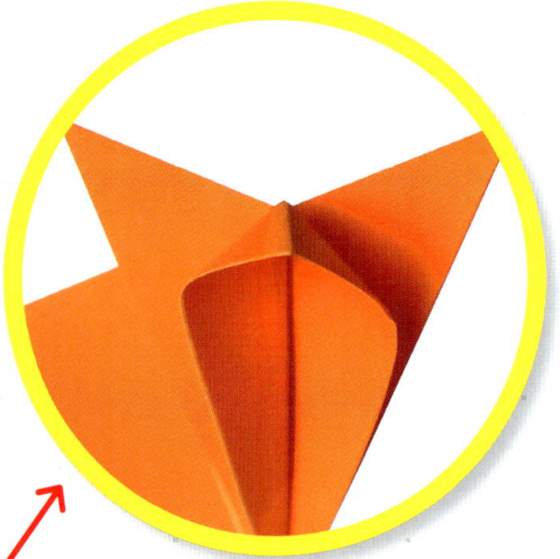

Here's a closer look at the squash fold.

DID YOU KNOW?

The arctic fox's fur is brown in the summer. It becomes thicker and changes to white in the winter. The winter fur keeps the fox warm and helps it stay **camouflaged** from **predators**.

7 Your model should look like this. Rotate your paper slightly to the left.

8 Valley fold the left point down to shape a tail.

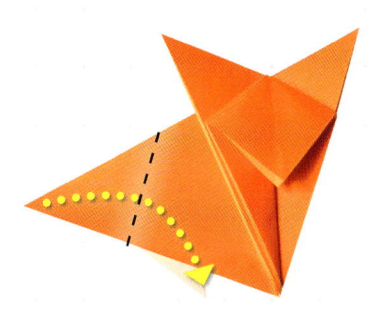

9 Valley fold the bottom point of the face up to make a nose.

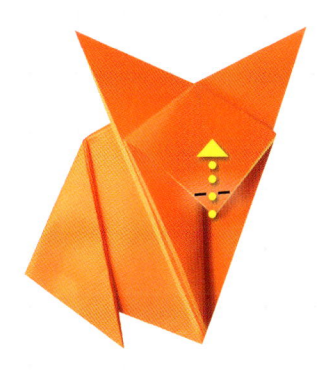

Next, you could use white paper to make an arctic fox in the winter.

9

Tundra Shrub

Shrubs are low-growing plants that are important to the tundra **biome**. They provide food for **herbivores** that might otherwise have a hard time finding a snack. Make a paper shrub for your origami tundra world.

1 Start with a kite base. Valley fold the center points of the upper layers out to the sides.

You will need
- 6 x 6 in. (15 x 15 cm) origami paper

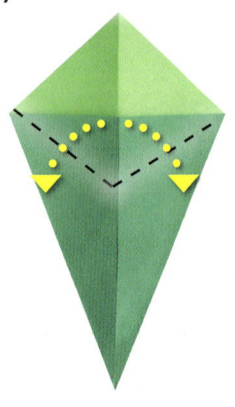

2 Your paper should look like this. Turn over your paper.

3 Make a pleat fold to the bottom of your model.

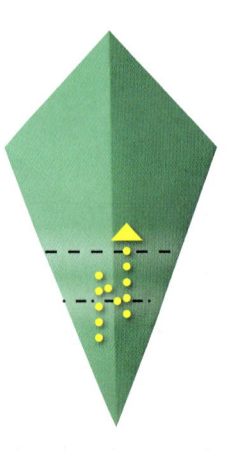

4 Make squash folds to the left and right sides of the top pleat fold.

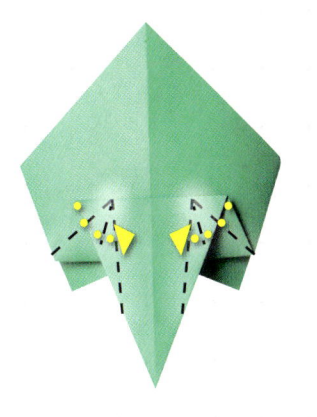

Here's a closer look at the squash fold.

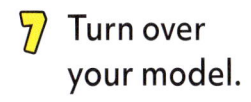

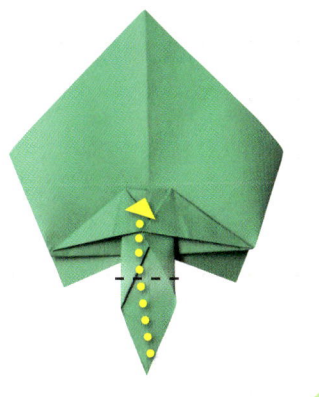

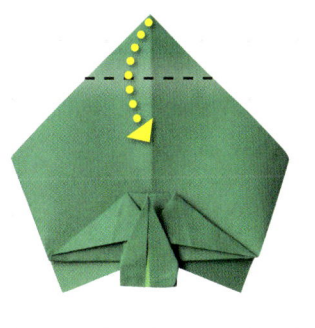

5 Valley fold up the bottom point.

6 Valley fold down the top point.

7 Turn over your model.

Place your shrub next to your tundra animals so they can have something to eat!

Snowy Owl

The snowy owl has **adaptations** that help it survive the tundra **climate**. Thick feathers cover its whole body to keep it warm. They even cover its feet and toes! Send your own paper snowy owl soaring.

You will need
- 6 x 6 in. (15 x 15 cm) origami paper
- Scissors

1. Start with a bird base. Valley fold the top layer to the bottom.

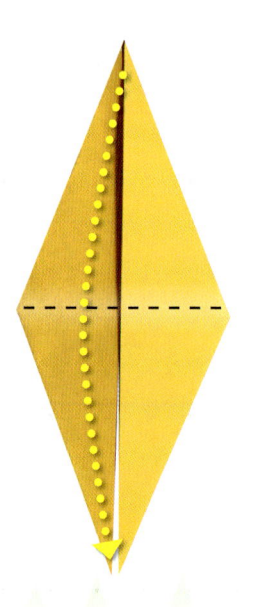

2. Mountain fold the taller layer of the top point.

3 Valley fold the upper layer of the left and right sides to the center.

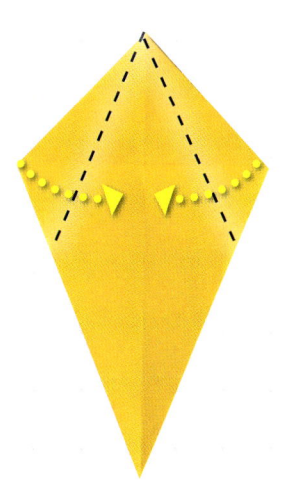

4 Mountain fold the remaining layer on the left and right sides.

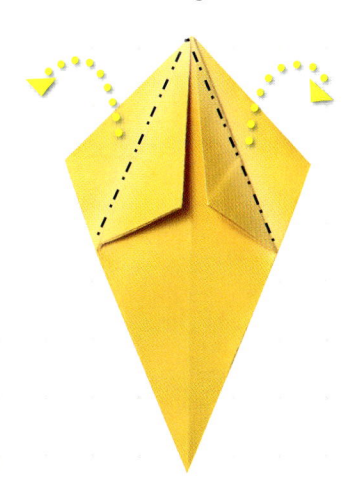

5 To create wings, inside reverse fold the left and right sides of the middle layer.

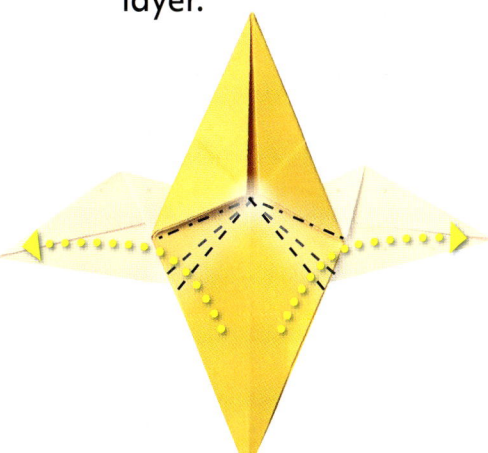

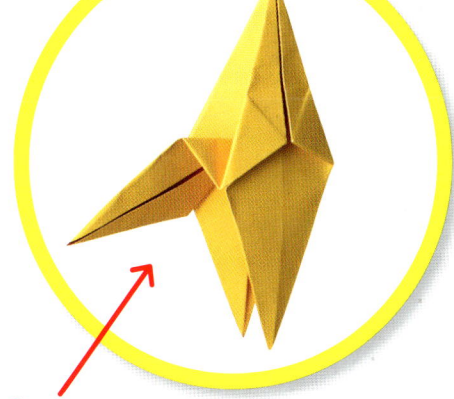

Check out page 4 to make sure your inside reverse fold is correct.

13

6 Your model should look like this. Valley fold down the top point.

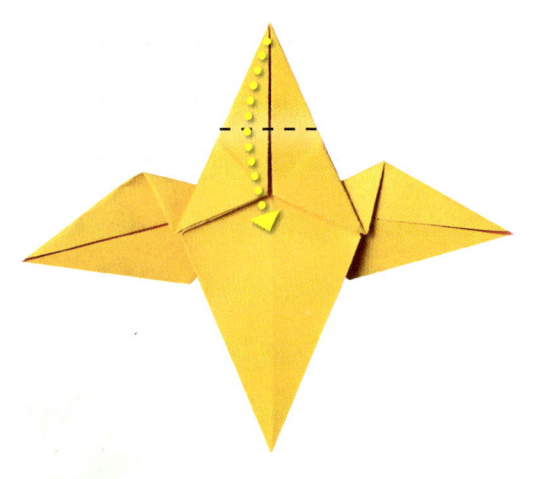

7 Make a pleat fold to the triangle created in step 6 to make the head and beak.

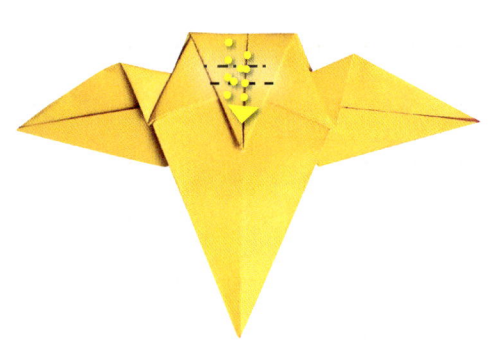

DID YOU KNOW?

Both male and female snowy owls have brown spots, but females usually have a lot more than males. The spots help camouflage the birds in tundra forests.

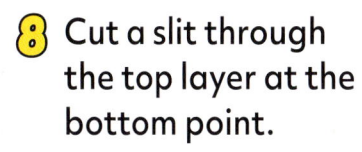

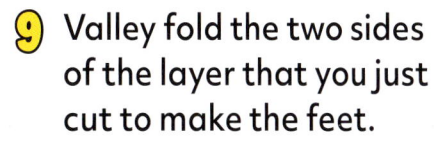

8 Cut a slit through the top layer at the bottom point.

9 Valley fold the two sides of the layer that you just cut to make the feet.

Cut very carefully.

Watch your owl fly through the tundra!

15

Pasqueflower

The **hardy** pasqueflower (PASK-flow-er) blooms in the tundra biome. With its purple-blue petals and yellow center, the pasqueflower is very pretty. But never pick a pasqueflower—it is **poisonous**. Instead, make this origami version, which will look just as cute in a vase.

1 Using one sheet of paper, start with a blintz base. Valley fold the inner points of the triangles out to the sides.

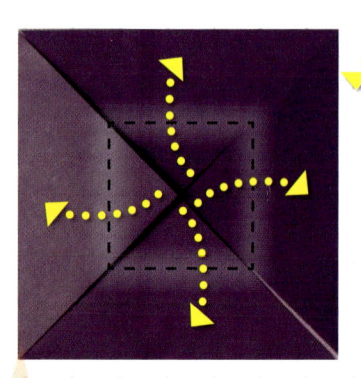

You will need
- 2 sheets of 6 x 6 in. (15 x 15 cm) origami paper
- Glue or tape

2 Mountain fold the four corners to finish your bloom.

3 Set this piece aside while you make the stem.

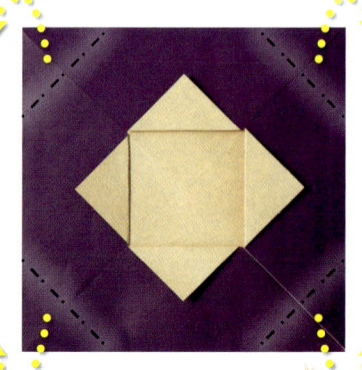

16

4. Take your second sheet of paper and start with a kite base. Valley fold the upper layer of the left and right sides in to the center.

5. Mountain fold your model in half.

6. Make an inside reverse fold to create a stem and a leaf.

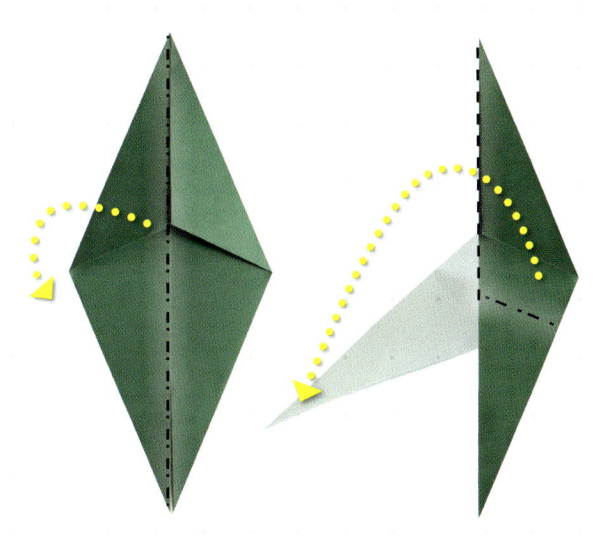

7. Rotate your model 180 degrees. Use glue or tape to attach your flower to the top of the stem.

Your bloom will last all winter.

Arctic Hare

Arctic hares have adapted to survive the cold tundra weather. They have thick fur and **burrow** underground to keep warm. Make your own paper arctic hare that's ready for the winter.

1 Valley fold the top corner of your paper to the bottom corner.

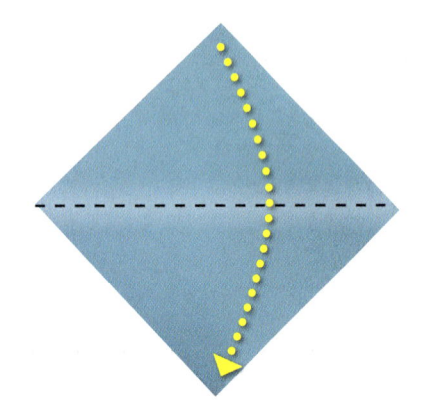

You will need
- 6 x 6 in. (15 x 15 cm) origami paper

2 Valley fold the left and right corners down to the center point.

3 Valley fold the left and right sides in to the center.

18

4 Make two squash folds to the left and right bottom flaps.

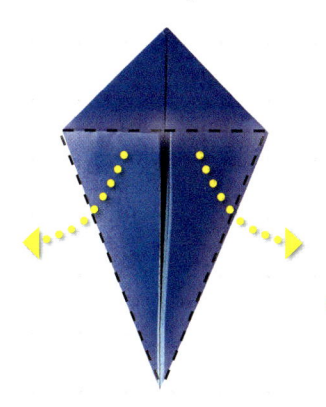

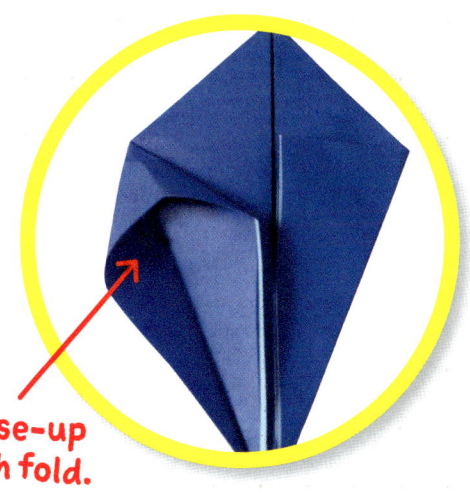

Here is a close-up of the squash fold.

5 Mountain fold your model in half.

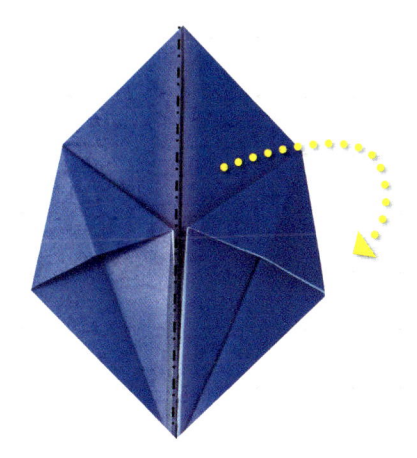

6 Rotate your model 90 degrees counterclockwise.

7 Mountain fold the right point up.

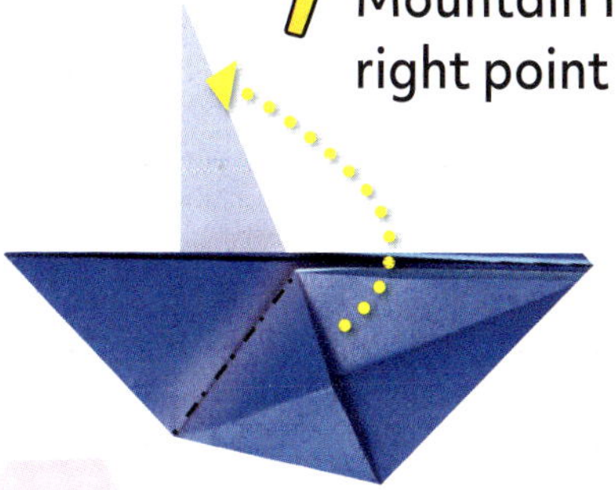

8 Valley fold the right part of the point to the left.

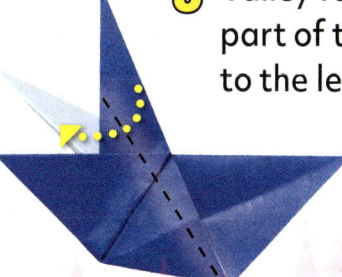

19

9. Your model should look like this. Turn over your model and repeat steps 7 and 8.

10. Your model should now look like this. The points will become ears. Rotate your model 45 degrees counterclockwise.

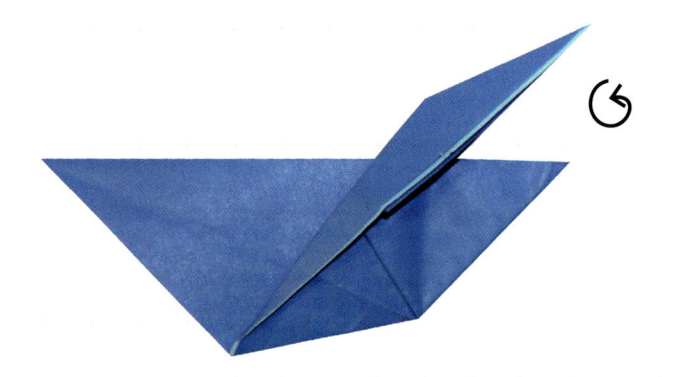

DID YOU KNOW?

Baby hares are called leverets. A **litter** of babies is born in the spring or early summer. There can be up to eight leverets in one litter.

20

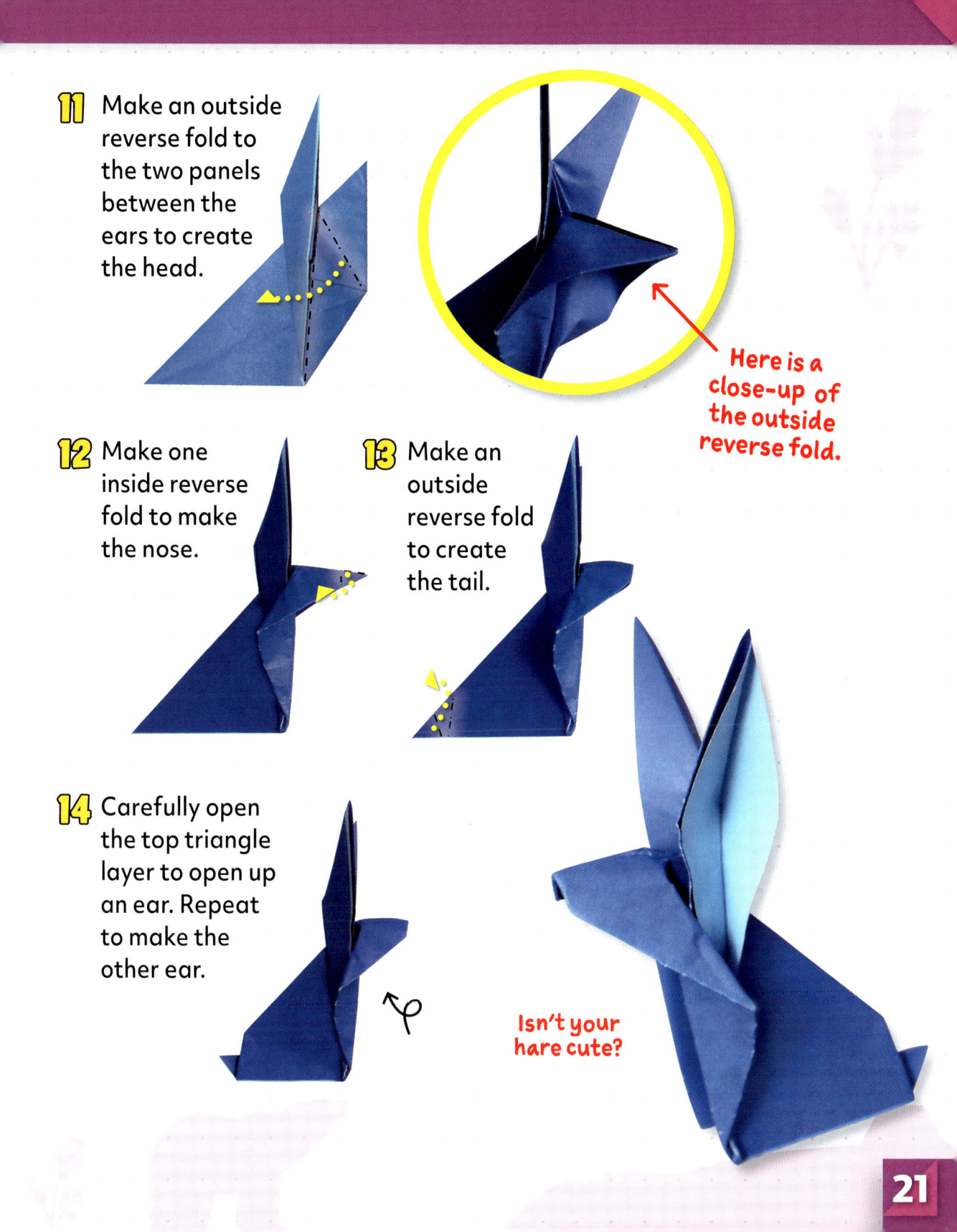

11 Make an outside reverse fold to the two panels between the ears to create the head.

Here is a close-up of the outside reverse fold.

12 Make one inside reverse fold to make the nose.

13 Make an outside reverse fold to create the tail.

14 Carefully open the top triangle layer to open up an ear. Repeat to make the other ear.

Isn't your hare cute?

21

About the Tundra

The tundra is the coldest of Earth's biomes. The average temperature in the tundra is around −18 degrees Fahrenheit (−28 degrees Celsius), but it can be much colder in the winter. It's so cold in the tundra that the top layer of soil is permanently frozen. Because of this, not many plants or animals live in the tundra. Those that do live there have special adaptations to help them survive.

Caribou, also called reindeer, are found in the tundra.

There is very little rain in the tundra, but there is a lot of snow!

Glossary

adaptations changes to animals or plants that help them survive in their environments

biome a region of the world with similar climates, animals, and plants

burrow to dig tunnels and dens underground

camouflaged hidden or blended in with the surroundings because of coloring or markings on the body

climate the typical weather in a region

hardy strong and tough

herbivores animals that only eat plants

litter a group of animals born at the same time

poisonous able to kill or harm someone

predators animals that hunt and eat other animals

tundra cold, treeless land where the ground is always frozen just below the surface

Index

adaptations 12, 18, 22
arctic fox 6–9
arctic hare 18–21
camouflage 8, 14
climate 12
herbivores 10
leveret 20
pasqueflower 16–17
predators 8
snowy owl 4, 12–15
tundra shrub 4, 10–11

Read More

Quinlan, Julia J. *What Is the Tundra? (Let's Find Out! Biomes).* New York: Britannica Educational Publishing, 2018.

Simpson, Phillip. *Tundra Biomes Around the World (Exploring Earth's Biomes).* North Mankato, MN: Capstone Press, 2020.

Learn More Online

1. Go to **www.factsurfer.com**
2. Enter "**Tundra Origami**" into the search box.
3. Click on the cover of this book to see a list of websites.

About the Authors

Jennifer Sanderson is an expert origami maker and author. When she isn't making origami, she is busy making other wonderful books for children. Jessica Moon is a paper engineer, illustrator, and designer. She loves making origami! Her favorite things to make are animals and beautiful flowers.